To

_____

From

_____

Date

_____

*The joy of the L*ORD *is your strength.*

Nehemiah 8:10

© Christian Art Gifts, RSA
Christian Art Gifts Inc., IL, USA
Printed in Vietnam

The LORD is my shepherd, I shall not be in want.

~ Psalm 23:1

_____

In all things God works for the good of those who love Him,
who have been called according to His purpose.

~ Romans 8:28

The eternal God is your refuge,
and underneath are the everlasting arms.
~ *Deuteronomy 33:27*

Be strong and courageous. Do not be terrified;
for the LORD your God will be with you wherever you go.

~ Joshua 1:9

You have made known to me the path of life; You will fill me with joy in Your presence, with eternal pleasures at Your right hand.

~ Psalm 16:11

As for God, His way is perfect; the word of the LORD is
flawless. He is a shield for all who take refuge in Him.

~ 2 Samuel 22:31

Ascribe to the LORD the glory due His name. Bring an offering and come before Him; worship the LORD in the splendor of His holiness.

~ 1 Chronicles 16:29

_____

The joy of the Lord is your strength.
~ *Nehemiah 8:10*

He will yet fill your mouth with
laughter and your lips with shouts of joy.
~ Job 8:21

O LORD, our Lord, how majestic is Your name in all the earth!

~ Psalm 8:9

The LORD will watch over your coming
and going both now and forevermore.

~ Psalm 121:8

_____

The heavens declare the glory of God;
the skies proclaim the work of His hands.

~ *Psalm 19:1*

The Lord is my light and my salvation – whom shall I fear?
The Lord is the stronghold of my life – of whom shall I be afraid?

~ Psalm 27:1

_____

One thing I ask of the LORD, this is what I seek: that I may
dwell in the house of the LORD all the days of my life.

~ Psalm 27:4

Taste and see that the LORD is good;
blessed is the man who takes refuge in Him.
~ Psalm 34:8

God has made everything beautiful in its time.
~ Ecclesiastes 3:11

_____

_____
_____
_____
_____
_____
_____
_____
_____
_____
_____
_____
_____
_____
_____
_____
_____
_____
_____
_____
_____
_____
_____
_____
_____
_____
_____

Praise be to the God and Father of our Lord Jesus Christ,
who has blessed us with every spiritual blessing in Christ.

~ *Ephesians 1:3*

_____

Finally, be strong in the Lord and in His mighty power.
~ Ephesians 6:10

Rejoice in the Lord always. I will say it again: Rejoice!
~ Philippians 4:4

Christ in you, the hope of glory.
~ *Colossians 1:27*

Now faith is being sure of what we hope
for and certain of what we do not see.
~ *Hebrews 11:1*

"Do not let your hearts be troubled. Trust in God; trust also in Me."
~ *John 14:1*

"Let your light shine before men, that they may see
your good deeds and praise your Father in heaven."

~ Matthew 5:16

_____

"Blessed are those who hunger and thirst
for righteousness, for they will be filled."
~ *Matthew 5:6*

"But seek first His kingdom and His righteousness,
and all these things will be given to you as well."
~ Matthew 6:33

_____

"Ask and it will be given to you; seek and you will find;
knock and the door will be opened to you."

~ *Matthew 7:7*

From the fullness of His grace we have
all received one blessing after another.
~ *John 1:16*

Shout for joy to the LORD, all the earth.

~ Psalm 100:1

Come, let us sing for joy to the Lord; let us
shout aloud to the Rock of our salvation.

~ Psalm 95:1

How many are Your works, O LORD! In wisdom You
made them all; the earth is full of Your creatures.
~ *Psalm 104:24*

The fear of the LORD is the beginning of wisdom;
all who follow His precepts have good understanding.

~ Psalm 111:10

You will keep in perfect peace him whose
mind is steadfast, because he trusts in You.

~ Isaiah 26:3

The LORD is my shepherd, I shall not be in want.
~ Psalm 23:1

_____

In all things God works for the good of those who love Him,
who have been called according to His purpose.
~ *Romans 8:28*

The eternal God is your refuge,
and underneath are the everlasting arms.
~ *Deuteronomy 33:27*

_____

Be strong and courageous. Do not be terrified;
for the LORD your God will be with you wherever you go.

~ *Joshua 1:9*

You have made known to me the path of life; You will fill me with
joy in Your presence, with eternal pleasures at Your right hand.

~ Psalm 16:11

_____

As for God, His way is perfect; the word of the LORD is flawless. He is a shield for all who take refuge in Him.

~ 2 Samuel 22:31

Ascribe to the Lord the glory due His name. Bring an offering and come before Him; worship the Lord in the splendor of His holiness.

~ 1 Chronicles 16:29

_____

The joy of the LORD is your strength.
~ *Nehemiah 8:10*

He will yet fill your mouth with
laughter and your lips with shouts of joy.

~ Job 8:21

O LORD, our Lord, how majestic is Your name in all the earth!

~ Psalm 8:9

The Lord will watch over your coming
and going both now and forevermore.
~ Psalm 121:8

_____

The heavens declare the glory of God;
the skies proclaim the work of His hands.
~ *Psalm 19:1*

The LORD is my light and my salvation – whom shall I fear?
The LORD is the stronghold of my life – of whom shall I be afraid?

~ Psalm 27:1

_____

One thing I ask of the LORD, this is what I seek: that I may
dwell in the house of the LORD all the days of my life.

~ Psalm 27:4

Taste and see that the LORD is good;
blessed is the man who takes refuge in Him.

God has made everything beautiful in its time.

~ Ecclesiastes 3:11

_____

_____

_____

_____

_____

_____

_____

_____

_____

_____

_____

_____

_____

_____

_____

_____

_____

_____

_____

_____

_____

_____

_____

_____

_____

Praise be to the God and Father of our Lord Jesus Christ,
who has blessed us with every spiritual blessing in Christ.

~ Ephesians 1:3

Finally, be strong in the Lord and in His mighty power.

~ *Ephesians 6:10*

_____

_____

_____

_____

_____

_____

_____

_____

_____

_____

_____

_____

_____

_____

_____

_____

_____

_____

_____

_____

_____

_____

_____

_____

Rejoice in the Lord always. I will say it again: Rejoice!

~ Philippians 4:4

_____

Christ in you, the hope of glory.
~ *Colossians 1:27*

Now faith is being sure of what we hope
for and certain of what we do not see.

~ Hebrews 11:1

"Do not let your hearts be troubled. Trust in God; trust also in Me."
~ John 14:1

"Let your light shine before men, that they may see
your good deeds and praise your Father in heaven."

~ *Matthew 5:16*

_____

"Blessed are those who hunger and thirst
for righteousness, for they will be filled."

~ *Matthew 5:6*

"But seek first His kingdom and His righteousness,
and all these things will be given to you as well."
~ *Matthew 6:33*

_____

"Ask and it will be given to you; seek and you will find;
knock and the door will be opened to you."

~ *Matthew 7:7*

From the fullness of His grace we have
all received one blessing after another.
~ *John 1:16*

Shout for joy to the LORD, all the earth.
~ Psalm 100:1

Come, let us sing for joy to the LORD; let us
shout aloud to the Rock of our salvation.

~ *Psalm 95:1*

_____

How many are Your works, O LORD! In wisdom You
made them all; the earth is full of Your creatures.

~ Psalm 104:24

The fear of the Lord is the beginning of wisdom;
all who follow His precepts have good understanding.

~ Psalm 111:10

_____

You will keep in perfect peace him whose
mind is steadfast, because he trusts in You.
~ Isaiah 26:3

The Lord is my shepherd, I shall not be in want.
~ Psalm 23:1

_____

In all things God works for the good of those who love Him,
who have been called according to His purpose.

The eternal God is your refuge,
and underneath are the everlasting arms.
~ *Deuteronomy 33:27*

_____

Be strong and courageous. Do not be terrified;
for the LORD your God will be with you wherever you go.

~ *Joshua 1:9*

You have made known to me the path of life; You will fill me with joy in Your presence, with eternal pleasures at Your right hand.

~ Psalm 16:11

_____

As for God, His way is perfect; the word of the LORD is flawless. He is a shield for all who take refuge in Him.

~ *2 Samuel 22:31*

Ascribe to the LORD the glory due His name. Bring an offering and come before Him; worship the LORD in the splendor of His holiness.

~ *1 Chronicles 16:29*

The joy of the LORD is your strength.
~ Nehemiah 8:10

He will yet fill your mouth with
laughter and your lips with shouts of joy.
~ *Job 8:21*

O LORD, our Lord, how majestic is Your name in all the earth!
~ Psalm 8:9

The Lord will watch over your coming
and going both now and forevermore.
~ *Psalm 121:8*

The heavens declare the glory of God;
the skies proclaim the work of His hands.
~ Psalm 19:1

The Lord is my light and my salvation – whom shall I fear?
The Lord is the stronghold of my life – of whom shall I be afraid?

~ Psalm 27:1

_____

One thing I ask of the LORD, this is what I seek: that I may
dwell in the house of the LORD all the days of my life.

~ Psalm 27:4

Taste and see that the LORD is good;
blessed is the man who takes refuge in Him.

~ Psalm 34:8

_____

God has made everything beautiful in its time.
~ *Ecclesiastes 3:11*

Praise be to the God and Father of our Lord Jesus Christ,
who has blessed us with every spiritual blessing in Christ.

~ Ephesians 1:3

Finally, be strong in the Lord and in His mighty power.
~ Ephesians 6:10

Rejoice in the Lord always. I will say it again: Rejoice!
~ Philippians 4:4

Christ in you, the hope of glory.
~ *Colossians 1:27*

Now faith is being sure of what we hope
for and certain of what we do not see.

~ *Hebrews 11:1*

_____

"Do not let your hearts be troubled. Trust in God; trust also in Me."
~ John 14:1

"Let your light shine before men, that they may see
your good deeds and praise your Father in heaven."
~ *Matthew 5:16*

_____

"Blessed are those who hunger and thirst
for righteousness, for they will be filled."

~ *Matthew 5:6*

"But seek first His kingdom and His righteousness,
and all these things will be given to you as well."

~ Matthew 6:33

_____

"Ask and it will be given to you; seek and you will find;
knock and the door will be opened to you."

~ *Matthew 7:7*

From the fullness of His grace we have
all received one blessing after another.
~ John 1:16

_____

Shout for joy to the LORD, all the earth.
~ *Psalm 100:1*

Come, let us sing for joy to the Lord; let us
shout aloud to the Rock of our salvation.

~ Psalm 95:1

_____

How many are Your works, O Lord! In wisdom You
made them all; the earth is full of Your creatures.

~ Psalm 104:24

The fear of the LORD is the beginning of wisdom;
all who follow His precepts have good understanding.

~ *Psalm 111:10*

_____

You will keep in perfect peace him whose
mind is steadfast, because he trusts in You.

~ Isaiah 26:3

The Lord is my shepherd, I shall not be in want.

~ Psalm 23:1

_____

In all things God works for the good of those who love Him,
who have been called according to His purpose.

~ Romans 8:28

The eternal God is your refuge,
and underneath are the everlasting arms.
~ *Deuteronomy 33:27*

Be strong and courageous. Do not be terrified;
for the LORD your God will be with you wherever you go.

~ Joshua 1:9

You have made known to me the path of life; You will fill me with
joy in Your presence, with eternal pleasures at Your right hand.

~ Psalm 16:11

As for God, His way is perfect; the word of the LORD is
flawless. He is a shield for all who take refuge in Him.
~ *2 Samuel 22:31*

Ascribe to the LORD the glory due His name. Bring an offering and come before Him; worship the LORD in the splendor of His holiness.

~ 1 Chronicles 16:29

_____

The joy of the LORD is your strength.
~ *Nehemiah 8:10*

He will yet fill your mouth with
laughter and your lips with shouts of joy.
~ Job 8:21

O LORD, our Lord, how majestic is Your name in all the earth!
~ Psalm 8:9

The Lord will watch over your coming
and going both now and forevermore.
~ *Psalm 121:8*

_____

The heavens declare the glory of God;
the skies proclaim the work of His hands.

~ Psalm 19:1

The LORD is my light and my salvation – whom shall I fear?
The LORD is the stronghold of my life – of whom shall I be afraid?

~ Psalm 27:1

One thing I ask of the LORD, this is what I seek: that I may dwell in the house of the LORD all the days of my life.

~ Psalm 27:4

Taste and see that the LORD is good;
blessed is the man who takes refuge in Him.

~ *Psalm 34:8*

_____

God has made everything beautiful in its time.
~ *Ecclesiastes 3:11*

_____

_____

_____

_____

_____

_____

_____

_____

_____

_____

_____

_____

_____

_____

_____

_____

_____

_____

_____

_____

_____

_____

_____

_____

_____

_____

_____

_____

_____

_____

Praise be to the God and Father of our Lord Jesus Christ,
who has blessed us with every spiritual blessing in Christ.

~ Ephesians 1:3

_____

Finally, be strong in the Lord and in His mighty power.
~ Ephesians 6:10

Rejoice in the Lord always. I will say it again: Rejoice!

~ Philippians 4:4

Christ in you, the hope of glory.
~ Colossians 1:27

Now faith is being sure of what we hope
for and certain of what we do not see.

~ *Hebrews 11:1*

_____

"Do not let your hearts be troubled. Trust in God; trust also in Me."
~ _John 14:1_

"Let your light shine before men, that they may see
your good deeds and praise your Father in heaven."
~ *Matthew 5:16*

_____

"Blessed are those who hunger and thirst
for righteousness, for they will be filled."

~ *Matthew 5:6*

"But seek first His kingdom and His righteousness,
and all these things will be given to you as well."
~ *Matthew 6:33*

_____

"Ask and it will be given to you; seek and you will find;
knock and the door will be opened to you."

~ Matthew 7:7

From the fullness of His grace we have
all received one blessing after another.
~ John 1:16

_____

Shout for joy to the LORD, all the earth.
~ Psalm 100:1

Come, let us sing for joy to the LORD; let us
shout aloud to the Rock of our salvation.

~ Psalm 95:1

How many are Your works, O Lord! In wisdom You
made them all; the earth is full of Your creatures.

~ Psalm 104:24